MEMORY TREES

--- family trees for the scrapbooker

some to
copy

some to
try

some to
inspire

Tony Matthews

CLEARFIELD

" GOING BOLDLY WHERE
NO FAMILY TREE
HAS GONE BEFORE "

Other books by Tony Matthews:

Paper Trees—Genealogical Clip-Art. Genealogical Publishing Company

Creativitree: Design Ideas for Family Trees. Using clip-art, magazines, photos, stencils, stickers...for both artists and non-artists as well. Clearfield Company

Printed for
Clearfield Company, Inc. by
Genealogical Publishing Co., Inc.
Baltimore, Maryland
2003

International Standard Book Number: 0-8063-5217-5

Made in the United States of America

MEMORY TREES *by Tony Matthews.*

So, you want to design your own family tree and feel creative, but you feel that you are not artistic enough......or at least not confident enough....? Do not despair ! Help is here !

In recent years there has been a huge increase in available art, mainly aimed at the scrapbook and memory album market. This stuff is widely available at arts and craft stores, school shops, office suppliers, even supermarkets. Plus there are many magazines, books, courses, and tv shows on the subject. The thing is, all of these techniques and supplies are perfectly applicable to producing your own brilliant family tree without even having to pick up a pencil or paintbrush !

If you are not familiar with what is out there, then please take a look. There's such a plethora that the challenge is *not* to come home with enough clip art, stencils, borders, stickers, punches, fancy paper, etc. to create a dozen very different, but all beautiful, family trees.

I'll use my own designs as illustration, rather than other folks' products as that would entail pages of copyright and source info, plus you couldn't then copy them. However, my designs should enable you to start building up a picture of what you could do, and this creative visualisation is your first step.

The second step is to find the right theme for your Tree. There are 2 approaches, one being to use images that you personally like......*your* Tree about your family. The other is to look for images that represent your family.....your Tree about your *family.* In some cases this will be easy where, for example, you have several generations of farmers. This gives you a range of images from corn to tractors to cows to barns. Most careers, hobbies and interests come with a set of images. A medical theme might include clip-art of stethoscopes, syringes, bottles of pills, a nurse's uniform, a black bag, scalpels....and so on. You may need to work with several themes for different branches of the family: your grandparents may include a nurse, a banker, a farmer, and one into making quilts. Then you could use the 4 sides of your sheet of paper, the top, bottom, left and right, to show these different sides of your family. If you have one prominent member, then find an image to represent him.....say a tank for a military hero....and paste it under his picture or details, or draw the silhouette and paste his name and details inside it. There is nothing difficult in doing a Tree, just a little thought in organising it, and if you are using "found" art then you don't even have to be artistic at all. It really is as simple as finding the right pictures and pasting them on in an orderly fashion. I will be showing you various different styles that you could use. Some need a little more creativity than others, but the simplest ones really could be done by a child. Just have a try, most of the pictures can be found very cheaply ($10 for a clip-art cd with 2,000 images on it) so you can afford to screw up your first attempt and fling it at the cat....sorry, wastepaper bin......and try again. I'm betting that once you've managed one, you'll look at it and think hmmmm, what if I......and you'll do another. It is actually a fun, relaxing thing, like doing a jigsaw puzzle.

SHAPING UP.

We'll get into fancier themes later, and the different toys that you might get to play with....some of these latter can be explored if we start with the simplest Tree, just using photos and names.

Take a look at my layout. This is the generic, centuries old, simple style, in the basic 1 (me), 2 (parents), 4 (grandparents), 8...16....etc. traditional format. You could do it differently, if you clearly mark the connections and relationships, but most genealogists use and recognise 1,2,4,8. Until scientists perfect cloning and genetic stuff where folk have 3 mothers (and forefathers !) we can assume this applies to everyone. More on this later.

The straight lines represent names, and the crosses are where photos go. You could copy this as your guide, or use a light box in a copyshop......it shines a grid through your paper, helping you to paste things on straight. So, here we go for a step by step. Please remember to put the words "acid-free" before any supplies....paper, pen, paste, etc. Most scrapbook stuff is, but you might want to sound knowledgable and ask the assistant.

FIRST STEPS

Let's start with the paper itself.......well, now, hold on. That would be simplest, but the more adventurous amongst you might even consider using an antique mirror, or a panel of weathered fencing. Then there's the quilters and sewers out there. If you consider that, for example, photos could be printed onto fabric (as you would for a t-shirt) then you could be doing a bedspread. Copy the photos, a bit of cotton stuffing under them, sew them onto a bed-sized cloth, add names written with a marker, or embroidered, on other pieces of fabric, some nice Belgian lace for the border.....and sew on and so on.

Okay, let's go the reasonable route and consider paper. White would work, but is just a little boring. Black could be really dramatic. Pale pink would be Victorian romantic.....let's go for that. But hold on, again, are we just going to have a plain colour ? I suspect not ! There are literally thousands of styles of printed designs available from the scrap book people. Then there is wallpaper (probably not acid free, but would last a good while, and a photo of it could last longer) and wrapping paper. Let's go for something with faded pink roses for a soft background effect.

You could get my layout printed onto it, or use a light box to mark the places, or simply collect your materials first and then lay them out, then juggle them around until they fit comfortably. The only thing to remember is the 1,2,4,8 format.

Let's tackle the border first (if you'd like one), as we will encounter many of the things that can also be used elsewhere on the tree. Borders can be pretty, a strong frame, contain pictures relative to the tree.....let me list some possibilities, some of which are just paste on, some may need a little practice first :

THE TOYS

Of course, you could just leave an inch preparatory to traditional matting and framing, but how about a bit of that Belgian lace.....?

You might consider embossing your paper.

There are designs on ink roller.

Then there are multitudinous stamps.

Clip art has a huge range of designs and pictures, floral, scrollwork, etc.

Maybe try a stencil.

You could cut stuff out of magazines.

Wallpaper and its decorative edging would be easy.

Scrapbook folk have many borders ready to fix on.

You can punch out shapes from paper....geometric, flowers, etc.

There are probably a thousand or two packets of stickers on every subject.

Ribbon could look pretty.

Those stick on jewellry bits your teenager uses.....

You can still get the old-fashioned transfers.

There are scissors that cut wavy and other fancy lines.

There are die-cuts either for the border, or large ones on the corners.

Would grandma mind you cutting up her old wedding dress ?...Probably yes, but the point is that you can use many kinds of paper, fabric, etc., either ready made, or by simply putting things in a line they will form a border.

IN THE PICTURE

I guess we should get some photos on now (copies, not originals !). These could be straightforward squares or rectangles, but there are little machines and dies to create round, oval, star-shapes, etc. Those fancy scissors could give an interesting effect. You can also get minature frames for each photo, or uses elements from the border. Let's say we found a nice wallpaper border with foliage and dark pink roses to complement our pale pink rose paper. Now I could cut out some of the leaves to edge the photos, or a single rose, with leaves, pasted on one corner.

NAMING NAMES

Then comes the names. You might want to include date and place of birth as well, perhaps date and place of marriage, maybe even a career or other distinguishing character.....though this is just a show piece, and you will have more information on these folk in your well organised files. So, shall we write the names on paper.....our desendants would appreciate seeing your own hand on this tree, as you would if you found one filled in by your great grandma, and acid-free pens are cheap and readily available with many different nibs etc......or we could type out the names in a fancy font on a computer or typewriter. We could use a complimentary or contrasting paper. I think I'll use a pale blue, oh, and those scissors again to give an interesting shape.....or perhaps I'll get a punch and make leaf shapes, that will go well.

FILLING IN

Hmmmm. Looking good, but there's still a lot of space between the photos. Let's look at that earlier list again.......yes, some stickers of red roses might complete the look, or maybe just a simple rose or leaf stamp in black or red ink would let the photos stand forward. Decisions, decisions. And just when you think you are finished, here I come again with another idea : how about fixing your tree at the back of a shadow box ? Now you can put in a lock of hair, grandpa's pipe, baby shoes, dress ribbon, ticket stub from a Beatles Concert, old Passport or Driver's License, mother's silver spoon..........

CHOICES

Family Trees can be serious, or fun, or gaudy, or works of art. Whatever you do will put a part of yourself into the Tree. And probably the kids or grandkids, they might enjoy picking out pictures, designs or stickers, and helping you paste them on. You can go for a floral look, they always seem to be popular, but if you are a nautical family then use ships, anchors, waves, flags, seagulls, fish....... the more specific to your family the better. You could even be more individual and find a sticker/stamp/picture that says something about each person.....a ship for uncle, a baseball for Johnny, a saucepan for ma, a saw for grandad, and something a little spicy for you-know-who. You're the one doing it, so you could just use things that you like, and when you look round the shelves full of scrapbook supplies you will find plenty that you do like.

You can be more generic, just using patterns, scrollwork, celtic knots, paisley, hearts, stripes, dots, etc., there's plenty around. Then there's stuff just to give an "old" look to your Tree with costumes through the ages, transport of the last thousand years, old tools and machines, various historical themes, or just old style pictures generally such as victorian. Any of this will give a nice feel to your design. If you are doing different Trees as gifts, then you might want to think about different styles that would appeal to each person.....gran might like flowers, your son might be into architecture, and your husband a sportsman. This approach will help to encourage them to keep....even display.... the Tree, things that will increase the chances of your material surviving.

What about Christmas, Birthdays, Graduation, Weddings, Reunions, Anniversaries.........? You get the fun out of creating a Tree, they get the pleasure of hanging it on their wall. assuming there's enough wall space in their restroom. No, they wouldn't, would they ?

CLUES FROM THE PAST

Still, at least the information has a better chance of surviving now....did I mention that was why we do Trees ? The historical documentation of families as a "Tree", and the recitation of pedigrees, are themes that go back into the mists of Time, and in many parts of the world, be it China, the Persians, Aztecs, Celts, Arabs, American Indians, Icelanders, Vikings......a common human trait. And why ?

Sometimes to prove descent from a warrior, or to show a valid claim to a throne, a title, or an inheritance. Marriage/mating featured too, and taboos about having children with a close relative are wide spread.....an instinctual breeding program ?

We can derive much from our ancestors, their traits, skills, achievements, medical history, culture and more, as well as having a lot of fun, (and some frustration!) doing the research. Plus we learn to understand ourselves better.

For a long time Trees were just that, a treeshape with names, or the straightforward pedigree chart or fan. There were also the Royal type where family coats of arms were illustrated. For the last couple of hundred years some Pennsylvanian/New England Germans have been producing frakturs, which are trees and various certificates....first hand done, later printed.......that featured some decoration such as flowers, birds and angels. Now we have such a huge amount of available artwork that anyone can use. Take stickers and clip art for example :

THEMES.

There are so many subjects possible, on a recent visit to a shop I saw

Trees
Flowers
Cars, planes, boats and trains.
The Southwest
Farm
Tools
Jobs
Machines
Toys
Circus
Seashore
Dinosaurs
Arthurian
Costumes
Space
Sci-Fi
Sports
Decorative scrolls, borders, patterns.
National, patriotic,flags, monuments, etc.
Music
Artworks

Stars, hearts, curves, paisley, and other shapes
Religion
Military
Alphabets
Animals, birds, fish and insects
Fruit
Architecture
Jungle
Dragons
TV and cartoon characters
Pop stars
Office equipment
Household gadgets
Party
Holiday, Christmas, Wedding, Graduation, Easter, Anniversary, etc.
Travel
Food
Theatre
Science
Landscapes
Celtic and other mythology
Hobbies
Gambling and lucky symbols
Figures from history
Communications
Zodiac

and more.

You should be able easily find images to represent and enhance your family and your tree. Again, I can only urge you to go and browse.

Next let's take a look at different shapes of trees. You need to put your names in an organised way, and are probably familiar with the pedigree chart that has you (or subject of tree, you might start with your child), then two parents, then four grandparents, and so on, with a layer for each generation. This gives you the basic 1-2-4-8-16-32-64-etc. layout that most folk will recognise. However, even within these tight guidelines, there is room for variation. I will show you some of my designs, in groups of similar patterns, with ideas on how to make your own. Most of my designs were drawn 10" X 10", which, with an inch border, will fit the standard 12" X 12" album. You are welcome to copy my picture for your personal use (though not for profit or gain), expanding them back to original size, but it should be much more fun to take the idea of the design and then recreate it using images more particular to you and/or your family.

HEARTS and ROSES.

Hearts and roses are always popular, and here you will see them used in a fan, a circle, and various pedigree styles, some that can be used in pairs as a his'n'her's. However, the heart could be replaced with any shape from the Toys and Themes list, as long as there is space to write the name etc. on. Thus it could be a dinosaur, a computer, a star, a ship......The roses could be any flower, using the Toys list, or any little image from Themes, as long as it is something that you like, or that represents your family.

You could do the whole thing on a pale patterned paper, and could also add a border, one that is a simple pattern, or one that contains more of the images that you've used already. Let's say that you used a picture of an old boat for your nautical or immigrant family, then your border might contain other ships, seagulls, fish, elements from the 'old' country, clips from a passenger list that mentions your ancestor, photos of them (there are machines that will copy photos right down to postage stamp size), and so on.

The boxes could have fancy cut edges, or a slim border, or have a small connected image that relates to an individual.

The other popular style of course is a tree, and as we have space here I will add HuMangrove, which is a tree, but reminds us that there is even a huge variety of actual tree shapes that could be utilised. I guess if you grew up in a swamp then this might be the perfect Tree for you.

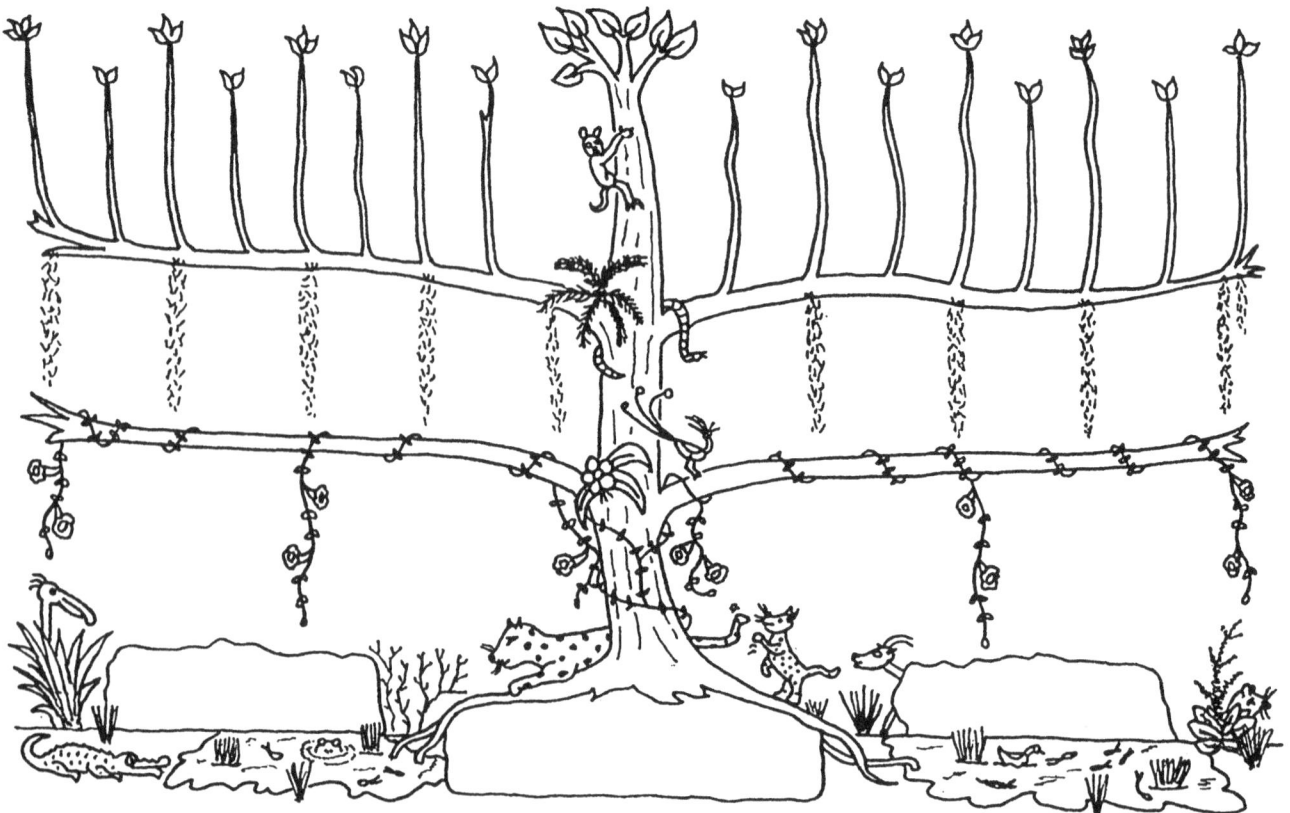

VICTORIA ROSE

© Tony Matthews 2002

FAMILY SPIN
© Tony Matthews 2003

HEARTFELT

© Tony Matthews 2003

RIGHT HEARTED
© Tony Matthews 2003

HEARTILY
© Tony Matthews 2003

UPPER HEART

© Tony Matthews 2003

BORDERS.

Borderland and Tribal illustrate two very versatile designs that only need pen and ruler and t-square (or graph paper makes it even easier). Here we have boxes either together, or opened up with spaces inbetween, and a border around them. Now you can give full rein to anything from the Toys and Themes list. Anything can work here, be it patterns or pictures, including the background. Tribal is a simple example of a family theme.....it was actually designed as a wedding present, and it is worth mentioning that the first square could be left empty for future children to be added in, or it could be used for the date and place of the wedding. Thus any of my designs could be for a wedding or anniversary, thereby celebrating the couple. I have filled one in for my wife and I, putting our company name in the first square. Of course any dog or horse breeders will already be familiar with pedigree charts, and Borderland (or several other designs) would work for them too, with the border used for photo+name of the animals, or photocopies of ribbons won, or clip art of horseshoes or pawprints !

Anyway, the hardest part on these 2 designs is deciding what images to use to represent you and your family......unless you do something patterned or historical....but most families have individual features, be it based on careers, hobbies, achievements, something ethnic, some favourite thing such as Art Deco, and so on. You can go for an overall theme, such as Tribal, or simply collect together various things to represent different ancestors. You will be creating something that is original and unique that tells of your family, says something about your creativity, and can be (copyright rules allowing) copied and passed on as an heirloom.

If you use clip art for your border, much of it is in black and white, but that needn't stop you from colouring in flowers, patterns, whatever. There are acid-free felt tips with a wide range of colours avalaible, plus metallic pens for interesting highlights.

Another simple use of this style is for cards and certificates. Take a 12X12 piece of paper (or letter size for a card), add a border, maybe with a little image in each corner, then type out your message or record.......Happy Birthday......Celebrating the Anniversary of.......Well done in your Exams......Enjoy your Retirement....Merry Christmas....and paste it in the middle of your decorated paper. There are many programmes and machines that will do cards and stuff, but how much nicer to get a personal home-made one.

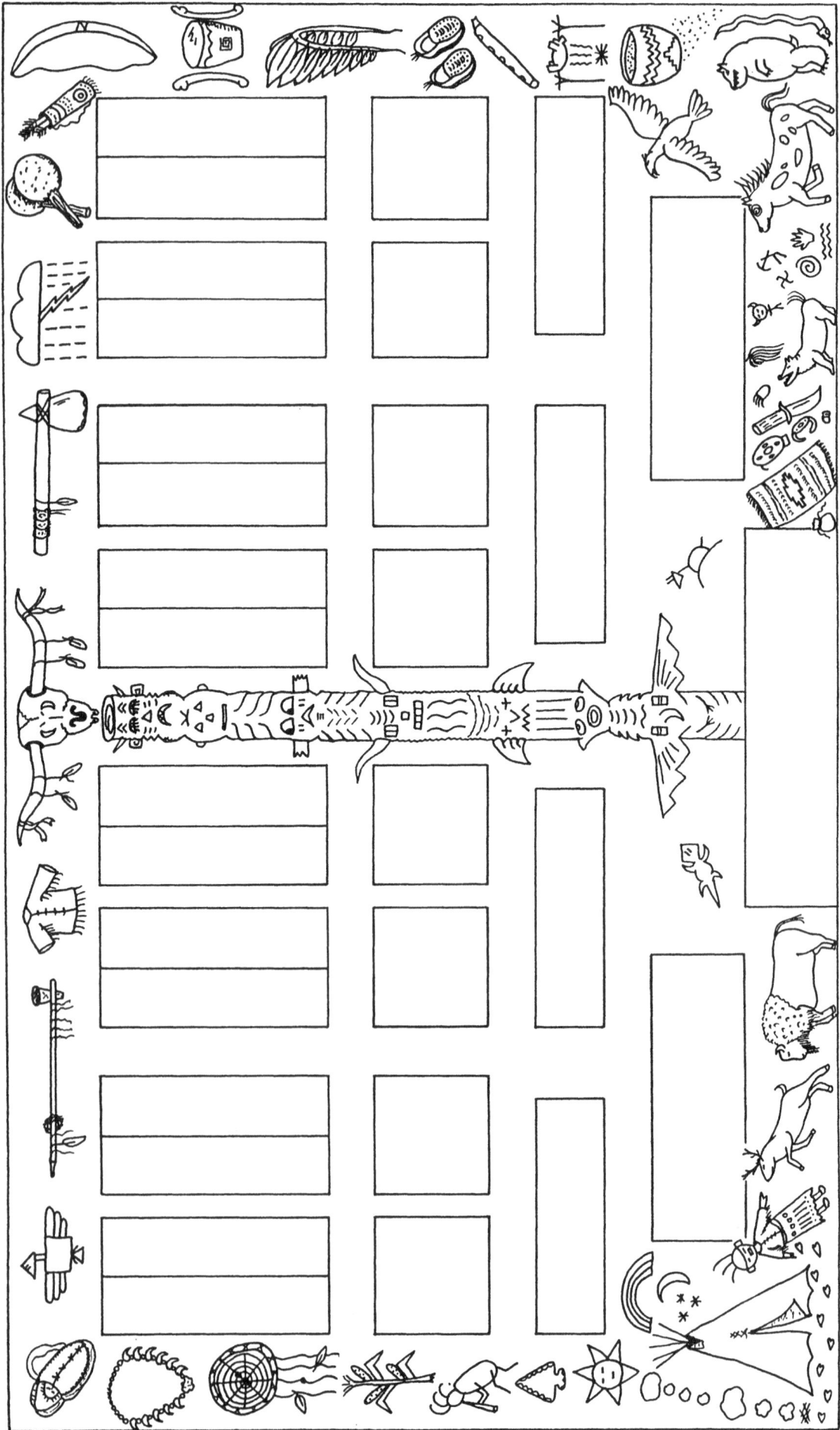

"TRIBAL"

BORDERLAND
© Tony Matthews 2003

JAPOP.

This is an accidental little design, but it neatly illustrates a style. It started out as a japanese garden with meditation tree, rocks for the names, and raked gravel........ but ended up more like a Mary Quant 60's style Op-Art design.

I'm using it here as an example of how to do a really simple tree, one that could be stylish or a fun one for kids to try. You start out with a sheet of boldly patterned paper.....wallpaper, scrapbook paper, wrapping paper.....or even a montage of different patterned pieces (similar colour ?) just cut ripped and pasted together overlapping, in a square panel, or cut square afterwards.

Then write/type your names etc. on paper, or fabric.....preferably a single colour to either compliment or contrast with the background (e.g. pale pink or blue on red). Next cut or tear off a name and paste it in place. A ruler will help to get an orderly effect, and remember the basic 1-2-4-8-16 format. Also remember that the name squares could actually be stars, leaves, hearts, wavy-edged, whatever.

A border would also be in order. Photos with name underneath would work well. Finally, a relevant image in the centre, like I used a tree, to gaze upon whilst you meditate on your family.

Then again, the focal point for meditation could actually be the whole thing, the outer shape rather than an inner one. We want our family to be remembered, and what better thing to use than the creature that never forgets. Also, if you grew up in India or Africa or a circus, then this little fellow might be appropriate for you too.

JAPOP
© Tony Matthews 2003

MIDDLE OUT.

Next we have some different designs where you work from the middle out. I have left these ones undecorated for clarity. The boxes themselves actually form a regular pattern, and I can see them as the basis for quiltwork, tiles, something in wood......?

Of course much can be added by the colour, shape and texture of the boxes, the background, and a possible border.

A family tree doesn't have to actually look like a tree, it is just an organised batch of information. As a contrast to the simplicity of the following "Middle Out" designs I will use the space here to present The 9 Sacred Trees Of Egypt. This is a playful little number, not seriously intended to be actually used, but it does help to show how Trees can be incorporated into a picture, rather than be the major part of it. No prizes for finding all 9, unless you count the raised awareness of possibilities.

9 Sacred Trees Of Egypt ?

© Tony Matthews 2003

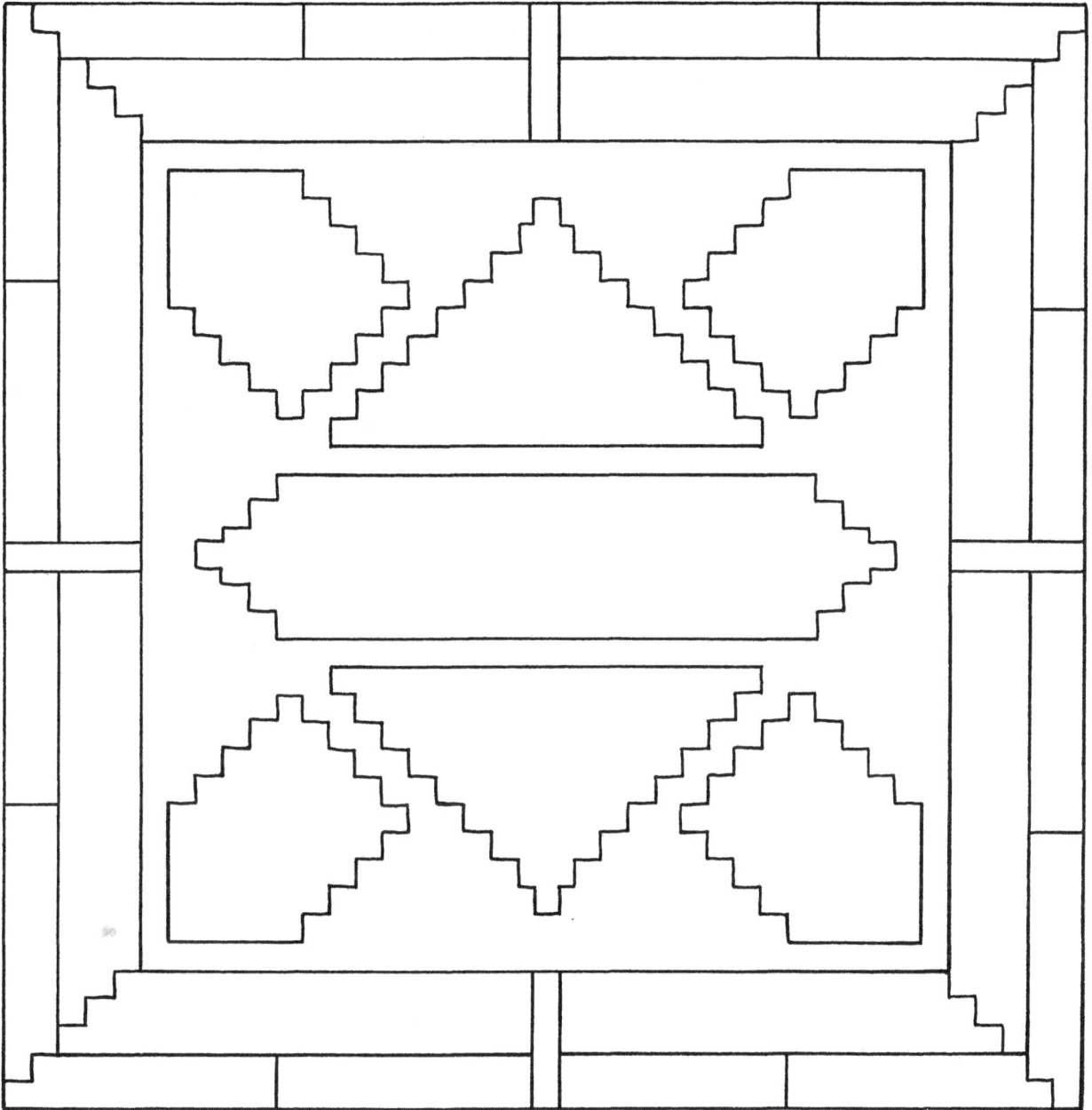

STEPS
© Tony Matthews 2003

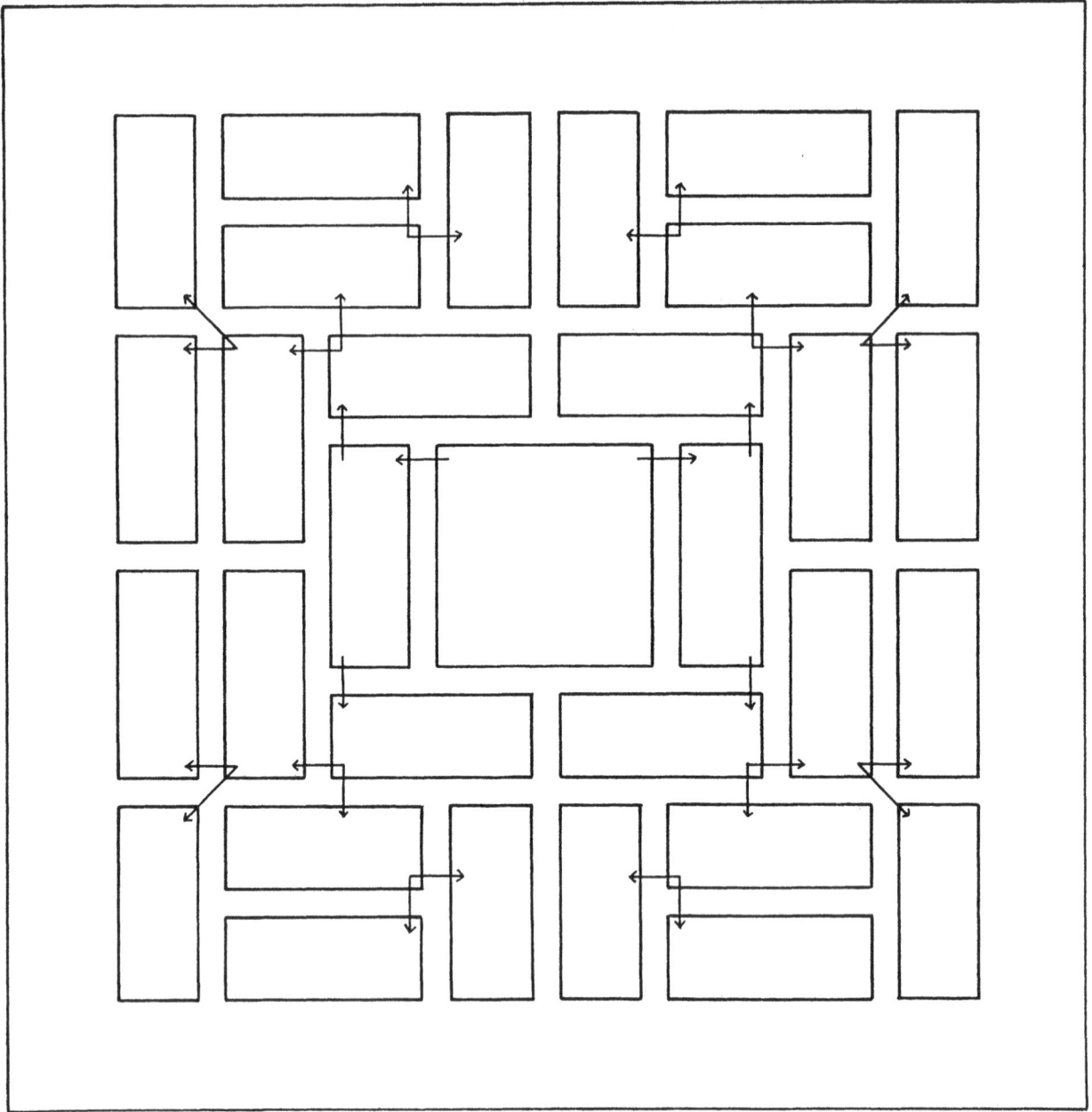

COURTYARD
© Tony Matthews 2003

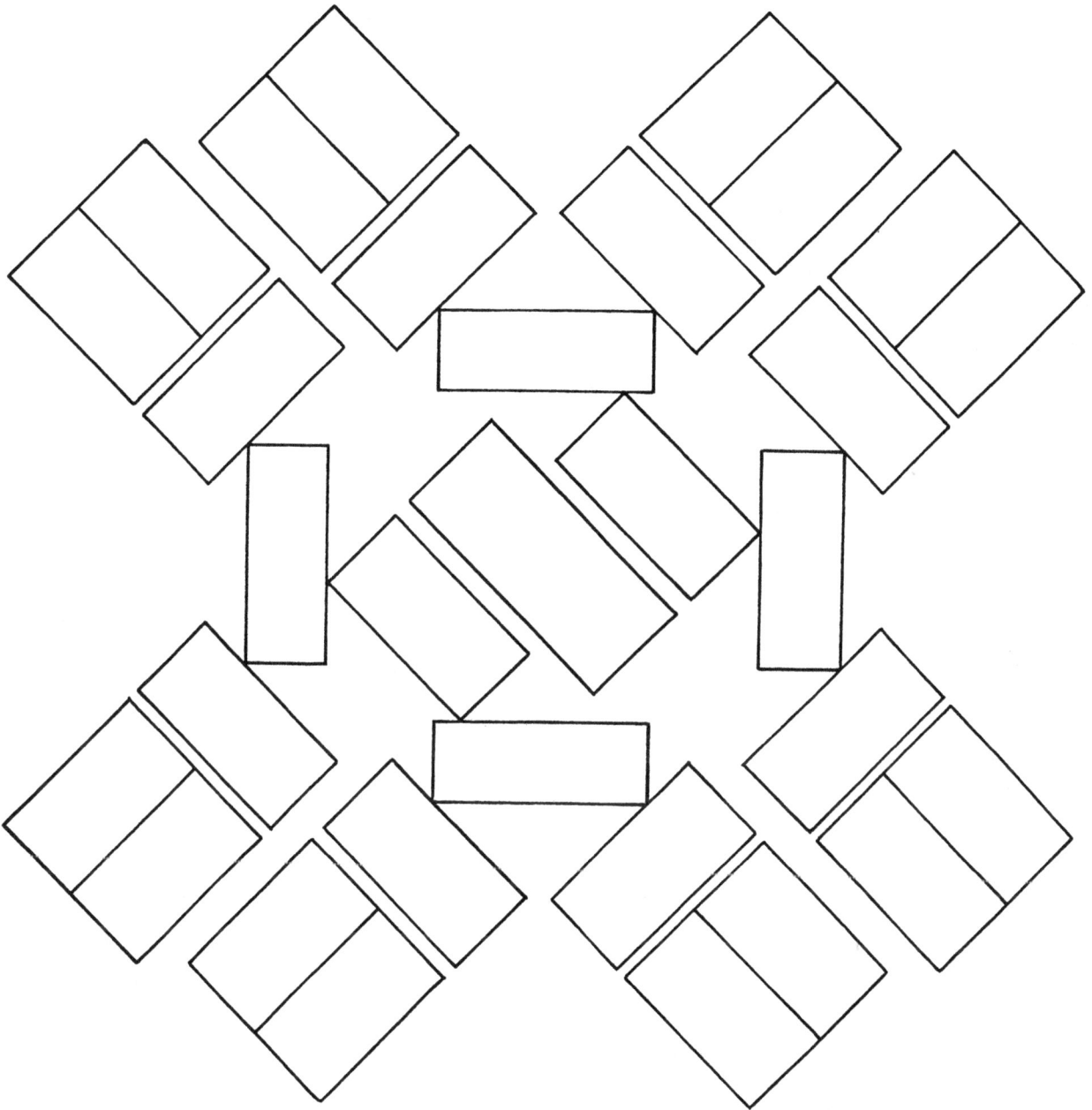

FLAGSTONES
© Tony Matthews 2003

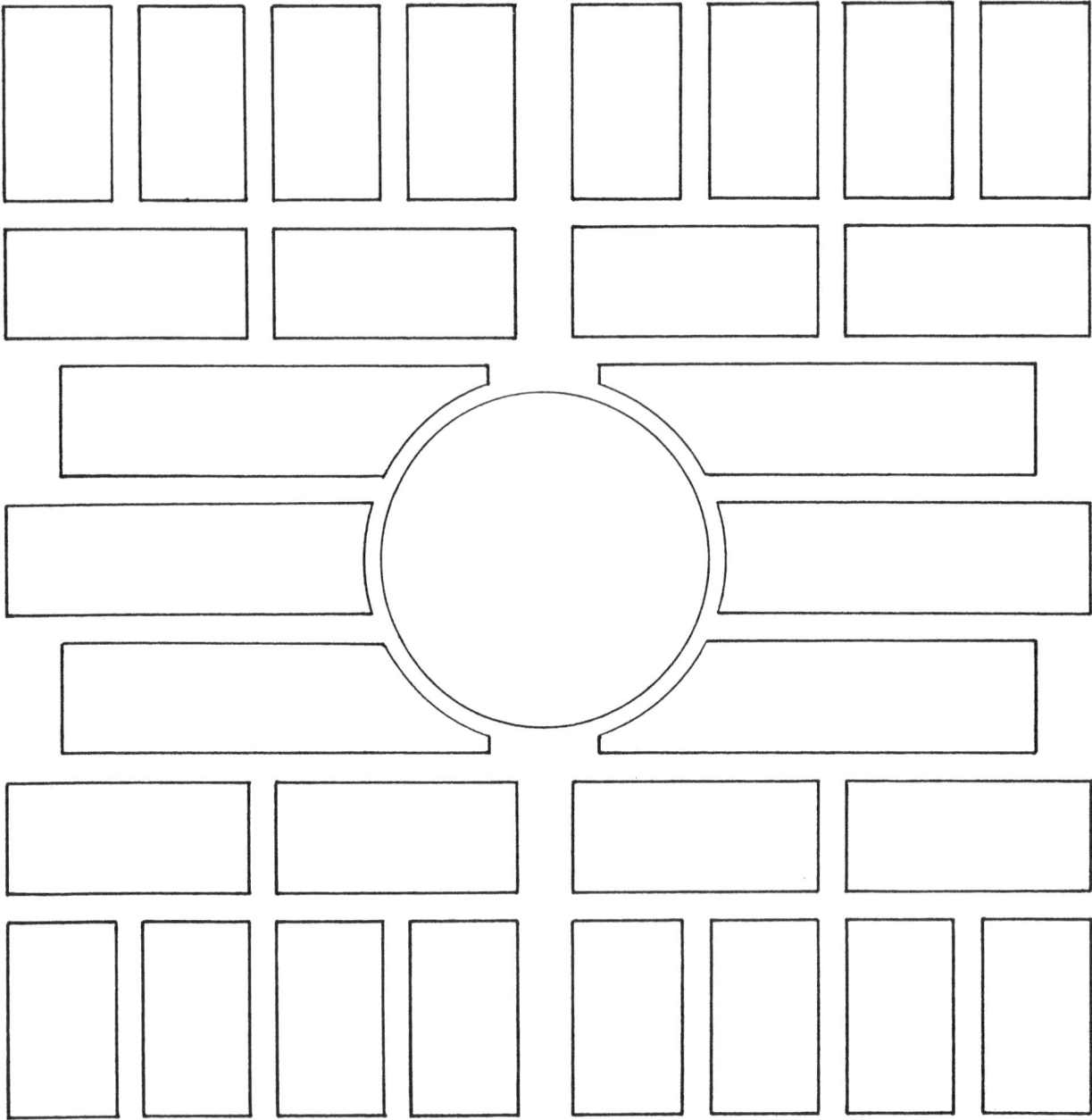

ORBIT
© Tony Matthews 2003

INTEGRATION.

So, boxes. Pretty boring sometimes. More interesting if given a shape such as a heart or a star, a ship or a dinosaur.......and then there's integration. In the following designs you will see that the square remains fairly squarish, but becomes an actual part of the picture as a cupboard door, a garden plot, a tent, etc.

What square shapes can you think of, or see around you ? Could they be incorporated into a Tree ? You don't need to be artistic to create one such as Ye Fayre, for all of the characters there could be found as stickers, clip-art, etc., and the tents (particularly if you use graph paper) are no great challenge to draw. Maybe you could do the tents, then let a kiddie loose with some stickers of cartoon characters ? Then as you, or he/she, write in the names it becomes a learning moment as you say a few words about each person.

You can buy a fancy ready-made Tree, such as I sell, and that's fine, but when you create your own, particularly if done as a family group, then it takes on a whole different aspect. Not only are you creating a family heirloom, and preserving and honouring your ancestors, but you are also passing on the knowledge (along with photos and stories), and creating a happy memory of the day itself. More, if a child helps with the project, is he/she more or less likely to discard the Tree itself ? Even if he/she finds it at the back of a drawer after you are gone, it will be doubly treasured, not only for the information and the beauty, but also as something that he/she helped to create. Even if you don't have kids, then drag in a cousin, sister or whoever you can, and make a happy day of it. The sharing of memories, facts, photos and stories over a cup of tea and biscuits (or several whiskies and a burger) whilst choosing pictures and creating a Tree together can be a wonderful experience....and further increase the chances of your family history surviving.

However, if you are the lone family historian, it can still be a great pleasure to create something beautiful, and useful, out of your hobby. You can still make copies, and create cards and certificates, to give to other family members. Don't despair, they are still likely to hang on to it, if only to not upset you ! Then it might be their child, or grandchild, that rediscovers it and maybe, just maybe, gets hooked. At least you will have done your share.

YE FAYRE
© Tony Matthews 2003

"OUR LITTLE CORNER" © TONY MATTHEWS 2002

OUR LITTLE CORNER
© Tony Matthews 2003

MONDAY MORNING
© Tony Matthews 2003

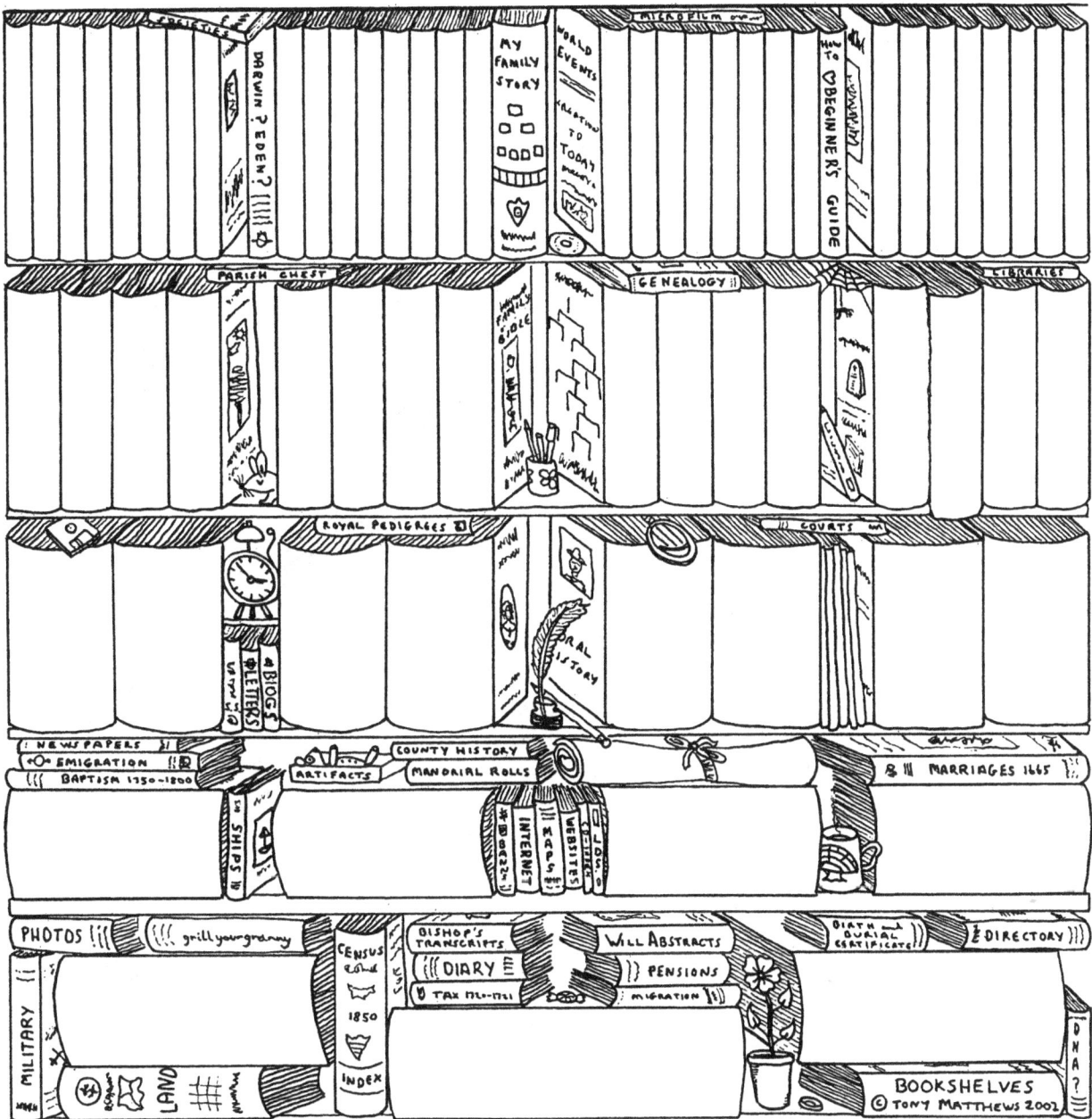

BOOKSHELVES
© Tony Matthews 2003

TREELER PARK
© Tony Matthews 2003

FOCAL POINTS.

You can incorporate as much or as little as you like into a design, and still be effective. It mostly relies on having a focal point. In the following designs Celtic Cross uses a lot of celtic imagery around the cross shape, but in Insect and True Hearts the central 3 boxes carry the whole design, whilst the rest of the boxes can be very plain. Graph paper is useful to set up these styles, and you could always go on to add a border.....could be a simple clip-art or wallpaper pattern, or more integrated such as bug stickers.

Trees have to be organised, as well as attractive, and thus art and science must meet. We have 4 grandparents, and a square has 4 corners, so from there out it is easy to get a regular pattern. It's the 3........or the 1 and 2 .....in the middle that is more difficult to arrange. You can, as in Celtic Cross, make a 4 in the middle, with the fourth arm being for the date and place of marriage, and the rest can flow naturally from there. Still, it's a challenge to come up with an idea for a 3 set.

Could we do chess pieces, with a king and queen, and a pawn ? Could it be 2 yachts and a canoe ? A shamrock ? A house and two trees ? A sofa and two armchairs ? Two triceratops and a T-Rex ? Two flowers and a heart ? An angel with two wings and flowing robe ? Think on....it's part of the fun, and if you are doing Trees as gifts then you might come up with something appropriate for each.

Genealogy isn't just about history and libraries and record offices and cemetries, it is about people, the living and the dead, and anything that people are interested in can be used as an appropriate Tree. Most jobs come with associated tools and products, most hobbies likewise, any interest from archeology to sports to science to travel comes with images, as do collections, cultures and religion. If you know anything about your people, then use an image with their name on your Tree to put some flesh on their bones......as they say, sometimes a picture can be worth a thousand words. Even if it's only worth a dozen, it still helps to tell the world, and your ancestors, more about your family.

The only other reason to explore your Past is to find out more about yourself from their traits, interests, medical history, and everything else that might be a factor in shaping your own character. A worthy search. And just once in a while someone will find out that they could be an Earl, or own half of London. You never know till you look.......

INSECT

marriage details

husband

wife

children

CELTIC CROSS
© Tony Matthews 2003

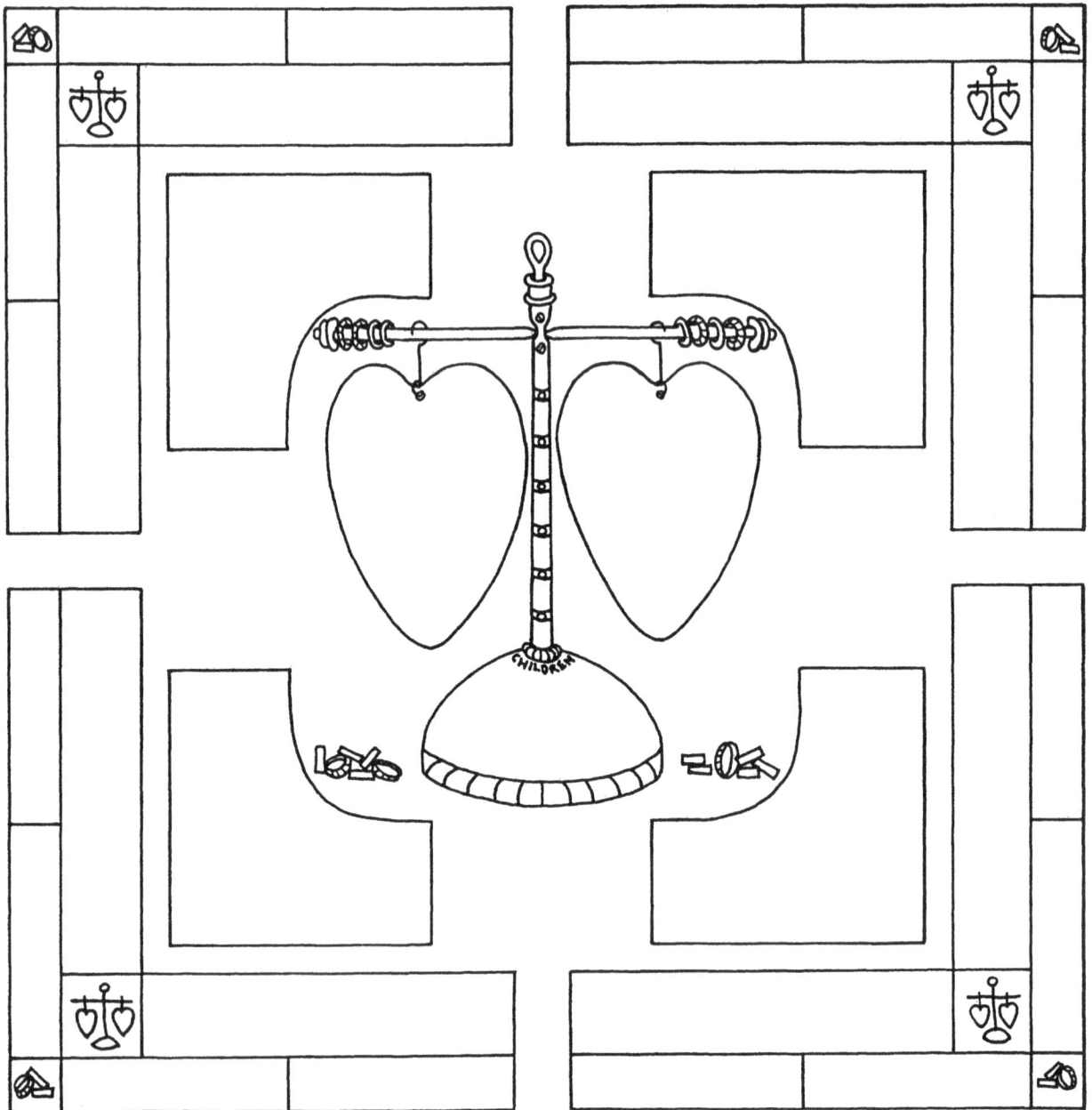

TRUE HEARTS
© Tony Matthews 2003

SHIELDED
© Tony Matthews 2003

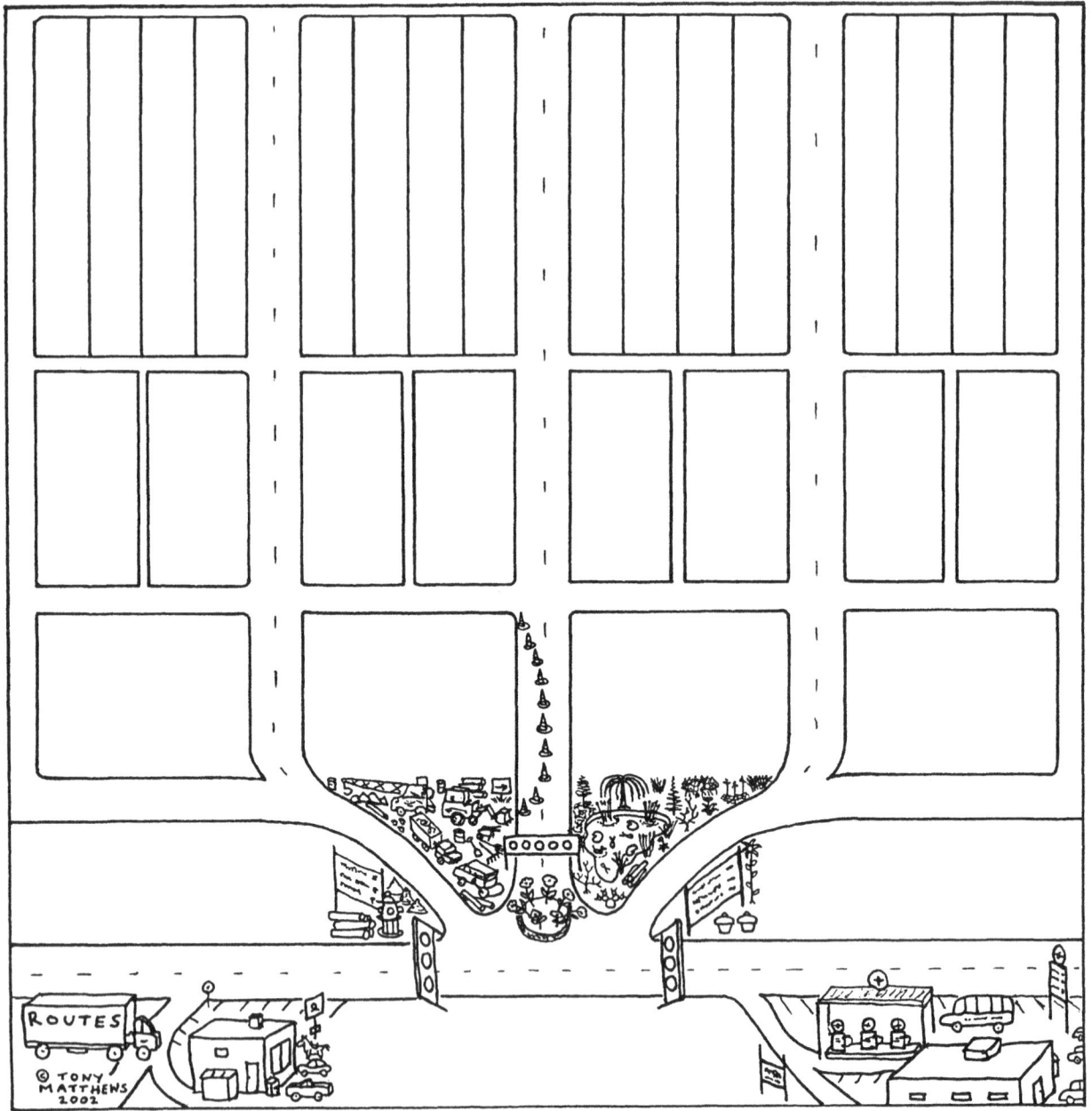

ROUTES
© Tony Matthews 2003

WRITABLE SHAPES.

Once you step away from boxes (which work perfectly well, but this is a creative book) and get into writable spaces you open up a whole new world. There are several different styles within this genre as well. You can simply past on pictures, leaving obvious spaces to add the names .....it's easier if you pencil in boxes first, add pictures, erase boxes.

You can use just one shape, for focal interest, then use regular boxes the rest of the way. Thus the hearts and roses style, it works real well.

Then there's the stack of similar shapes, it might be computers, trucks, dinosaurs, stars or hearts all the way.

And for the even more creative there's the different shape for each name, with the shapes adding up to a complete picture. All you need to remember is to keep it all orderly and 1-2-4-8.

Of the following designs, Reflections and Just The Tip, a sort of fire and ice, use irregular shapes suggesting rocks or icebergs. Not too difficult to draw the shapes, and figures can come as clip-art, stickers, anything from the Toys list....and a border could be added too.

Forest Floor sticks to the theme of leaves, but I've used a different shaped leaf denoting each generation. You could use any vaguely leafy/floral paper as a background, with the name leaves cut out of green or brown paper or fabric.
Various bugs, seeds, and such could come as clip-art, stickers, etc.

Or then they could be boats on a watery background, stars on blue, hearts on floral.......you might note that for easier following I have overlapped each leaf slightly on the two "parent" leaves.

Finally you can go all out with such as Toys and Top Gun, with all of the shapes different, but adding up to a whole. Not so easy, but a lot of fun.

When I first started looking at memorytrees for scrapbookers I was worried that the hardest part would be for folk to find a theme to suit them, but having looked at all of the wonderful available artwork, paper, tools and techniques....added to my own ideas and types of designs.... I think the hardest thing to do will be to stop with just one Tree ! How can this much pleasure still be legal ?

REFLECTIONS

© Tony Matthews 2002

REFLECTIONS

© Tony Matthews 2003

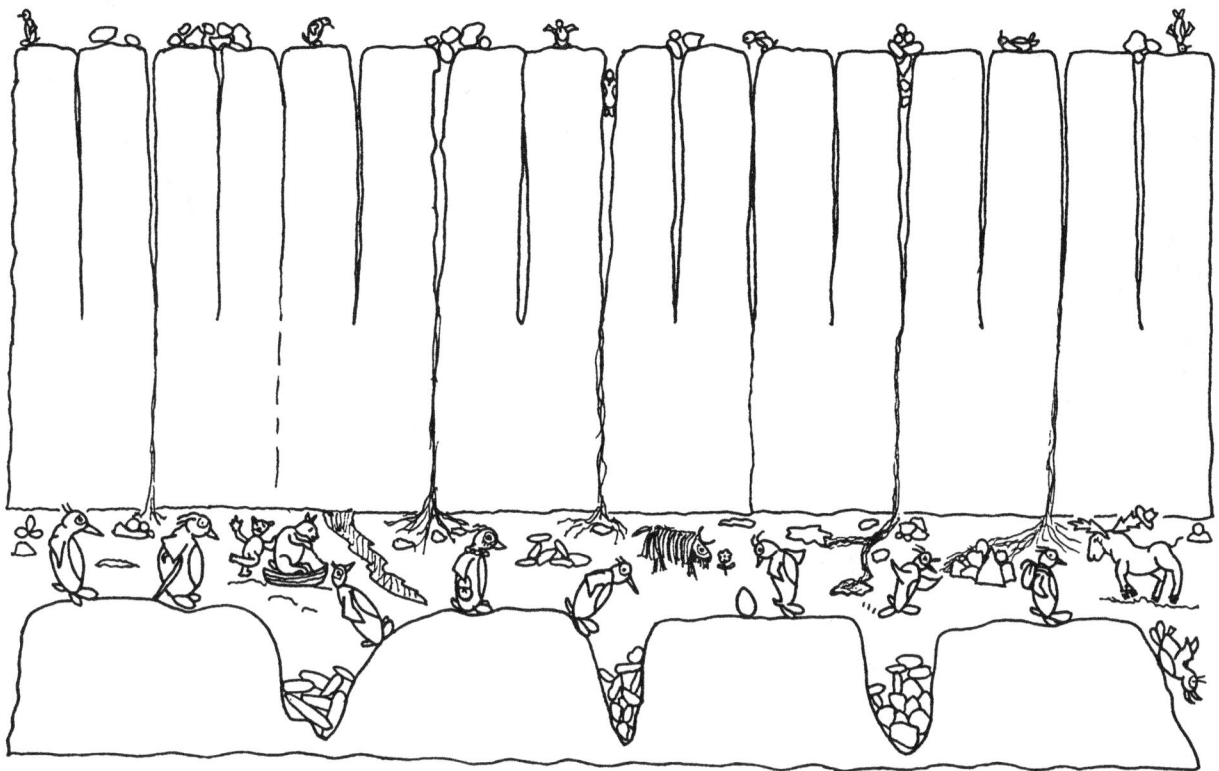

JUST THE TIP
© Tony Matthews 2003

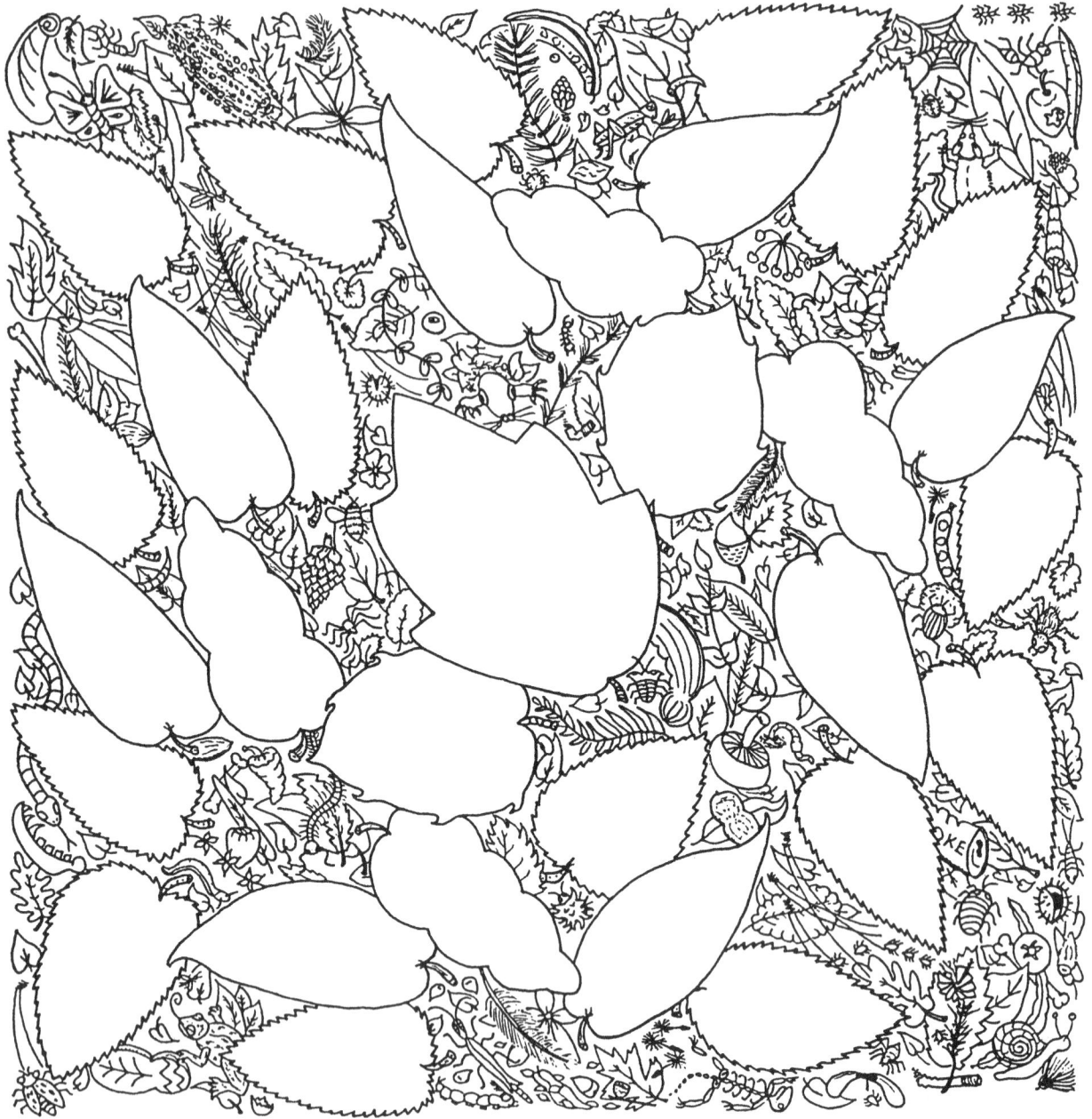

FOREST FLOOR
© Tony Matthews 2003

TOYS
© Tony Matthews 2003

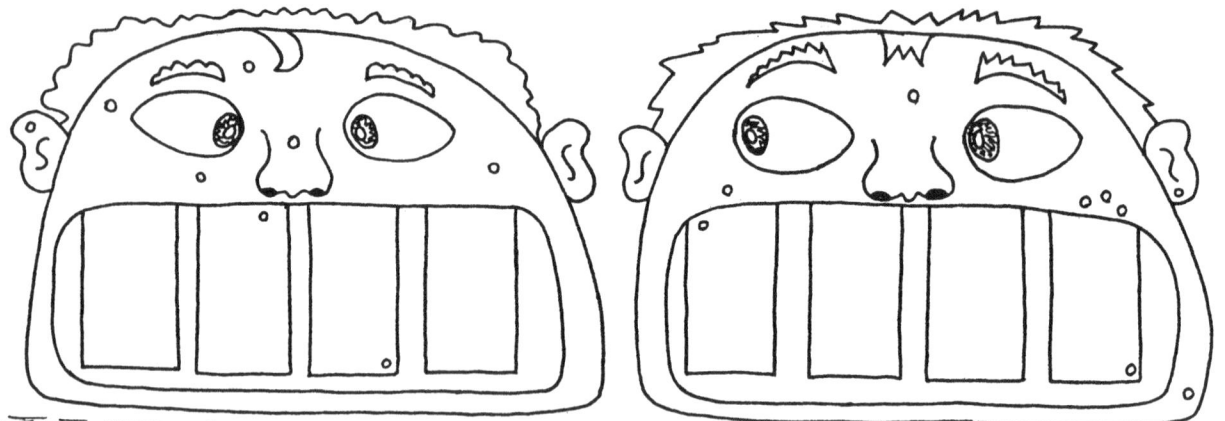

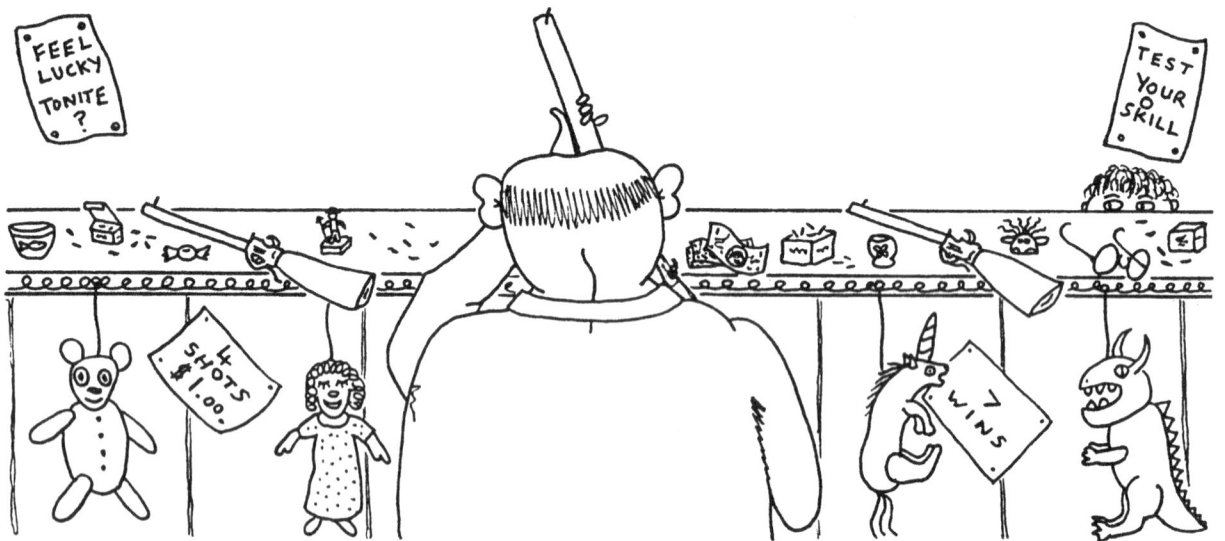

TOP GUN
© Tony Matthews 2003

MORE COMPLETE.......

If you are doing a complete Tree with everyone, aunts, cousins and in-laws' in-laws on it, then you can still add images in the invariable spaces, or with each person. Plus a border, of course, with anything from the Toys and Themes lists.

An interesting half-way style is the Siblings Tree. This is in fact a simple 5 generation Tree, but with a space beside each person for their siblings, as these naturally have the same parents. Their desendants will also have shared ancestors.

Another useful Tree is for adopted folk. Now, you could use a regular Tree, and end up with a lot of blank boxes, with the hope that you will eventually be able to fill them in. But it is also possible to juggle things around to give a complete looking Tree. I am often told by someone that it's not worth doing a Tree for them as they, or a parent, are adopted. However, the people saying this have a spouse and children, who certainly do have a Tree, and the adopted person is a branch, albeit a short branch, on that Tree.

In the 2 examples (no decoration so that the style shows clearly) I have started with

a) the child(ren) of an adopted person. The adopted person is there in place, and carefully marked. His spouse and her ancestors then fill the rest of the Tree.

b) is a person who had an adopted parent. We start with his children, then him and his spouse, then spouse's parents and his own with the adopted one clearly marked. The next generation then fills the Tree with the parents of the 3 that are known....these are 6 out of the 8 grandparents of the children of a guy with an adopted father (you can swap genders around for whoever was the adopted person).

I have still based it on the 1-2-4-8 system, and it is a good exercise for the future when we deal with 3 parent families, clones, and such where it might need a 1-3-5-11 or some other weird combination.

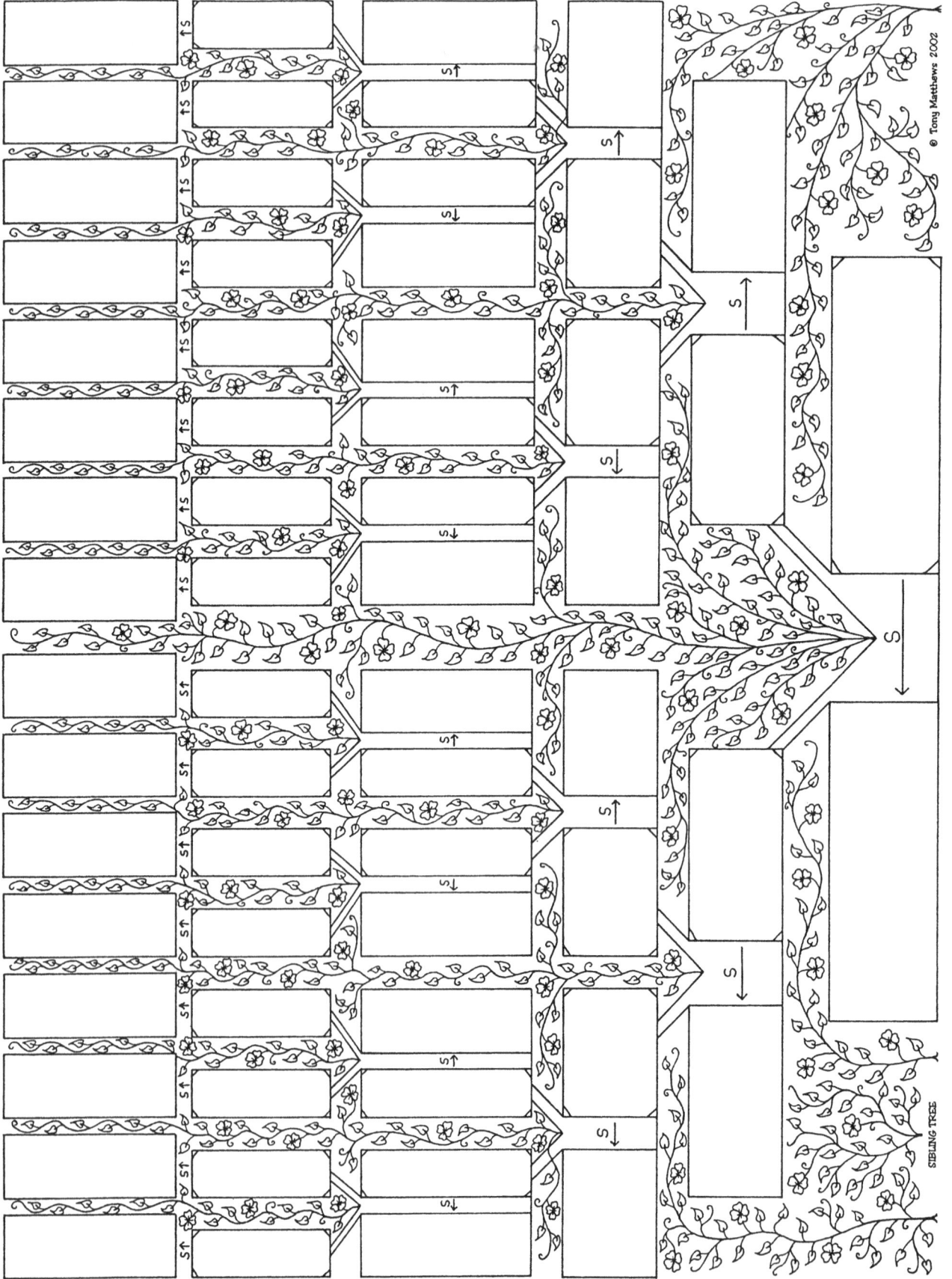

SIBLING TREE

© Tony Matthews 2002

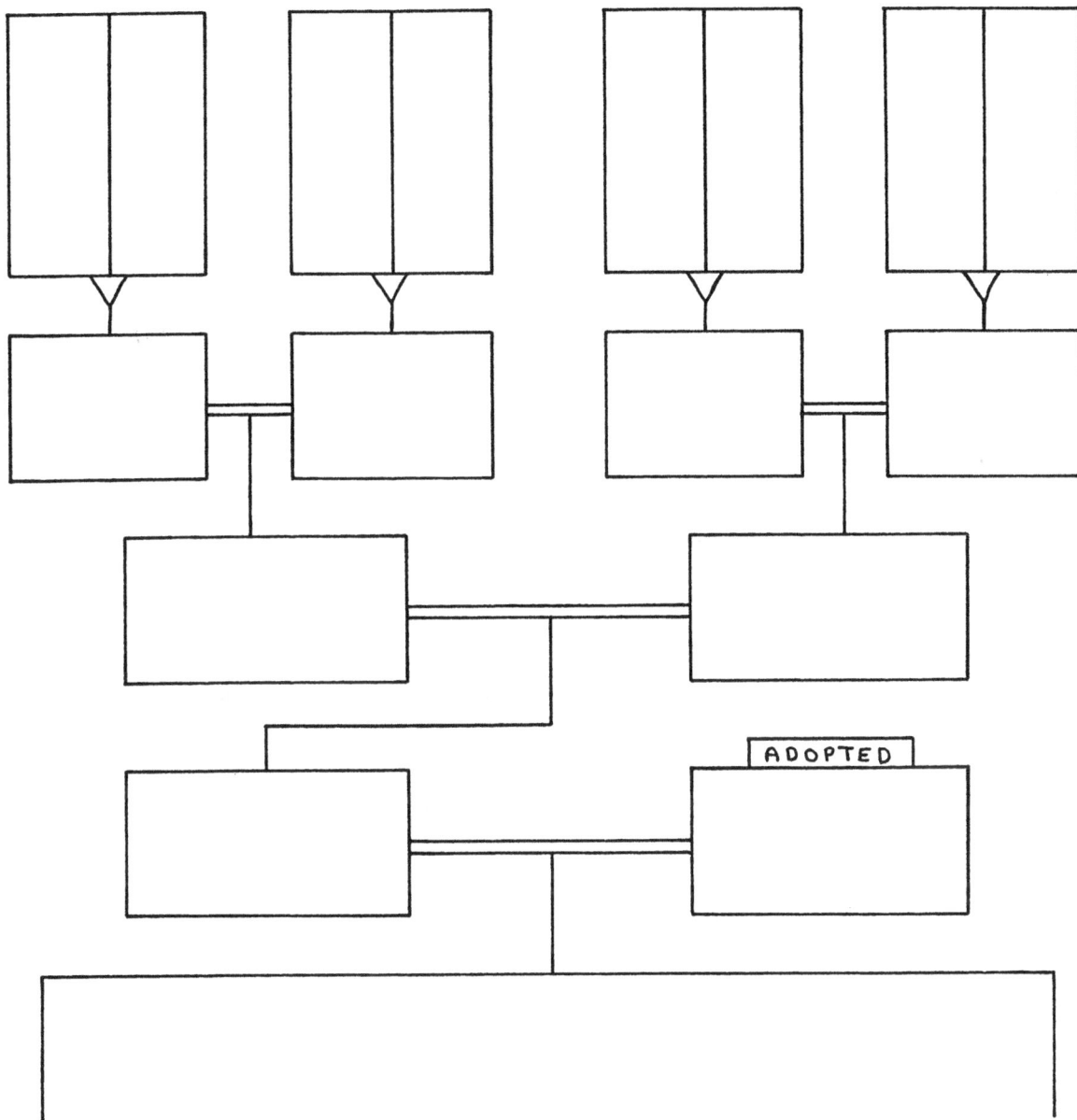

ADOPTED

© Tony Matthews 2003

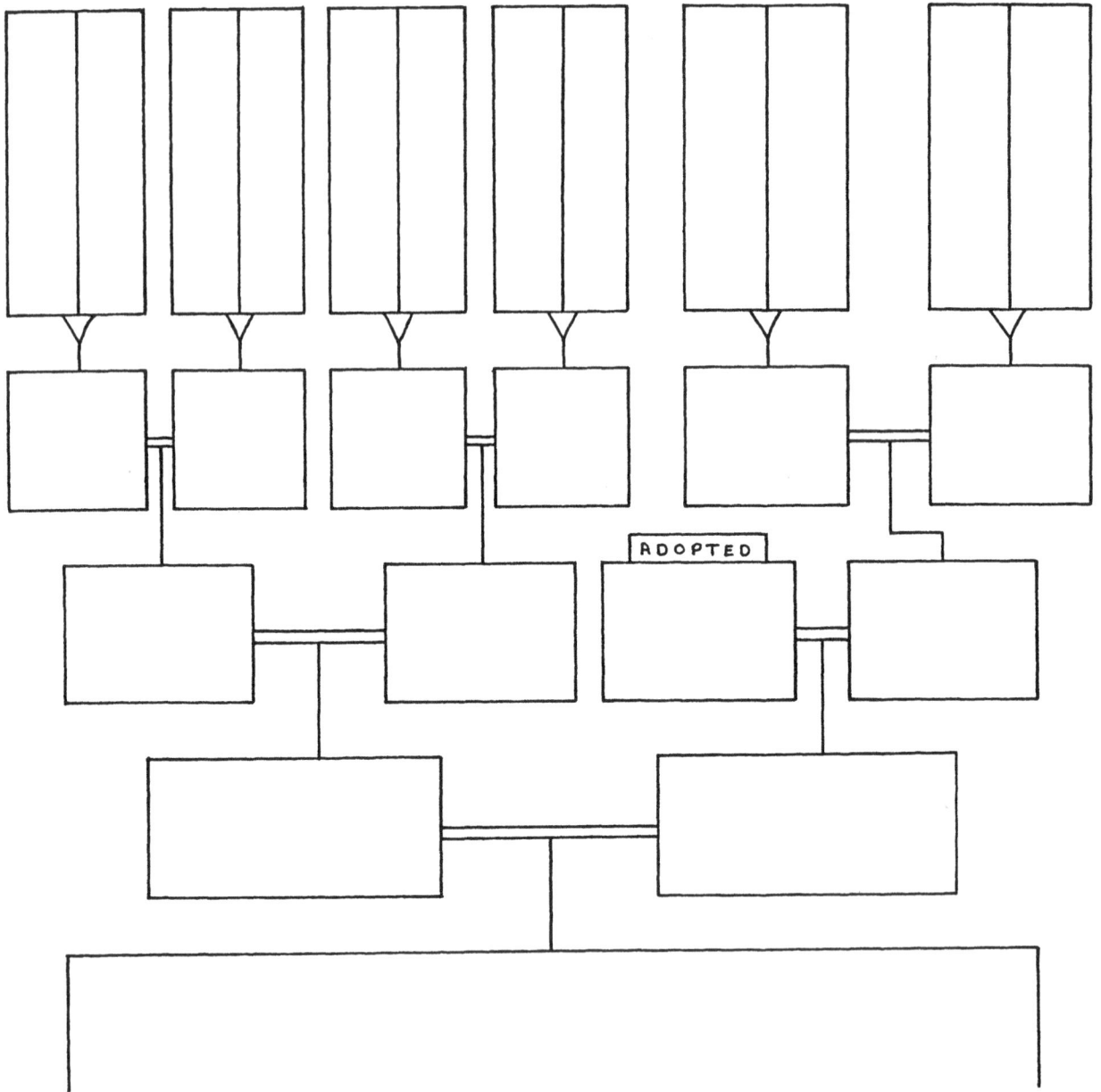

ADOPTED PARENT
© Tony Matthews 2003

WHAT NEXT ?

Genealogy spends a lot of time looking backwards to the Past. When we draw up a Family Tree in the Present we are also then thinking of the Future, and the preservation of our family history. The main purpose of this book has been to help you create your own Tree, and this will become even more important in the Future, for things are stirring............though there are various Trees available, they are all in the 1-2-4-8-16 format, even my huge collection. This will suffice just for now, but we are entering a world of science fiction turned reality. I am talking about various forms of genetic engineering, DNA research, cloning and such, that are with us right now, and will affect our desendants, and yes, even Family Tree designing.

We have the first children with DNA from 2 mothers already with us, the first reports of cloned humans filtering in, and more. All ethical, legal and moral considerations aside, you can be fairly certain that this stuff will continue and grow. Anyone drawing up a complete Tree, with all ancestors, aunts, cousins and in-laws should be able to gather in the various strands, as they have always done, and the Family Historian can absorb all of the variations into their story, but for genealogists, and pedigree situations, and printed 1-2-4-8-16 Trees and charts then it all changes. Many will be affected, from the whole legal side of Wills and Inheritances, to the clerk who has to come up with new Birth, Marriage, and just about every other Form and Certificate that asks for details of parents. You will see what I mean as we explore some of the new possibilities already available :

What's Happening ?

We can now get children with 1, 2, or 3 parents (so "forefathers" is barely a joke). Much of this has stemmed from research into infertility, as well as some diseases and illnesses. Let's look at 2 mothers first......it's a technique called ooplasmic transfer. If you think of a woman's egg as if it were like a chicken's (no offense intended), then in the white of the egg you find little power packs called mitochondria. If these are defective then the egg doesn't activate. So, they extract these little batteries from another woman's egg, and insert them into the first's. Okay, now the egg is viable, however, within those transferred mitochondria are some DNA from the the second lady, and these will turn up as a germline of genetic material in the female child. Et voila, 2 mothers. I don't know what this child would then pass on to her own children, but let's consider something else.

The one parent child. Sperm is no longer necessary to fertilise an egg. In fact, men are obsolete in a potential world of women only. They can now fertilise the egg with genetic material from any part of the body, though the result is always a female child. However, this means that we can use the woman's egg, and if hubby is infertile, we can use any part of him to get some genetic material, and thus they can have their "natural" child. Sounds good so far, but this also means that a lesbian couple could have a child, and more......a woman could have her own baby, just a reproduction of herself. A one parent child. Let's take another step forward :

Me, Me, Me.

The ultimate in ego gratisfaction must be the clone. Just reproduce yourself, no body else needed. Now, it will be an interesting part of a family history, but genealogically speaking (and Treewise) how do we handle it. Who are the parents ? Are the clones more like brothers or sisters ? There could be up to 100 years difference in their age, which might distort the records somewhat, and make research more difficult. What will a Birth Certificate say ? If that clone comes from someone with 3 parents, then our Tree starts to lean sideways !

Not that a clone would ever end up just like you, for it is born into a whole different world of family, school, culture, world events and more. Imagine yourself growing up without, say, World War 2, or with having a home computer to play with instead of going fishing or skipping in the streets. (the above will sound pretty dated in a generation or two, but should still be a good illustration, even though a more appropriate one by then might be "imagine growing up on Earth" !).

Baby, it's cold outside.

Yes, and inside too, when we go on to consider frozen embryos. The possible permutations (or should that just read mutations ?) continue to extend into time and space. With apologies to anyone who has been in this situation....Here we can get into half-mothers as I introduce you to Adam and Eve, a nice little couple who get wed, and try for a baby. And try again. And try again. Seems little Evey has infertile eggs, or something, but thanks to modern science they can use some of Adam's sperm, somebody's mitrochondria here, a bit of someone else there....well anyway, they get half a dozen fertilized eggs, pop 4 in the fridge next to the yoghurt, and the other 2 back in Eve. One works, and they have a strapping young son Noah. Don't put away the hankies yet.

At Noah's second birthday party Adam chokes on a piece of birthday cake, and dies. Life goes on. Eve brings up Noah on her own for a few years, but, do you know, she gets lonely. Now, she is not going to be unfaithful to poor Adam, no, she is make of sterner moral fibre than that. Then one day, when she is cleaning out the fridge she notices a little box at the back, next to a carton of green yoghurt. Of course, 4 eggs !

Well, they are part of Adam after all, so she warms one up in the baby bottle warmer, and pops it in herself (it's probably more difficult than that, but you get the idea). Soon she is cuddling the cutest little baby girl, Rebecca, who has her father's blue eyes and green hair (or maybe it was the yoghurt ?). The records will show Rebecca as being born several years after her father died. Hmmmm. Eve still has some fertilised eggs that her mum and dad had done (her mum having the same problem) and she wonders, just wonders, what if........

Perhaps her mum being the clone of a one parent child was a factor, but life is not always fair. Get a clean hanky, and we'll try a different time-line. This time, it's Eve that get's the cake.

Adam manfully brings up young Noah on his own for a few years, but it's a lonely life......until he meets the lovely Mary with the mini skirt in the office. She looks into his sad young /old eyes, and they end up married. They try to have their own baby. And try again. And again. It's fun, but they are getting nowhere. One day when she is cleaning out the fridge she comes across a little box......She asks Adam about it, he tells her that they are fertilised eggs. "Oh" she says, clutching them to her bosom " I swear I can feel them thawing out already." " Hey," says Adam, "They are actually half me. Would you like to get them installed ? Oh, and can you throw out that yoghurt while you're there ?"

To cut a long story short they soon have a bonny girl Elizabeth and a green-haired boy Hercules. Not twins, just born the same day, and that being several years after their mother died, though we can't forget Mary, though I don't know where she goes on the Birth Certificate. Maybe she uses Eve's cake recipe one day, and then we lose her too. Now we're down to 2 eggs, and need a new box of tissue.

But there's hope yet. Adam had always fancied his cousin Matilda. She is now recently bereaved too. Of course they can't marry, but living together....well. One evening, sitting in front of the fire, eating fresh yoghurt, Matilda tells of her life, and how she is sorry that with her defective womb she was never able to give her husband any children. Adam looks at the yoghurt pot, and ponders.....plastic hearts, liver transplants, inflatable boobs......he makes some phone calls, and soon a womb donor is found. Matilda is a little delicate yet for getting babies the old-fashioned way, so one of the last 2 eggs is thawed out.....I've lost count of mothers, where were we ? Oh, yes, egg from Adam and Eve, was it ? Womb from unknown (any DNA contribution there ?), all put into a third "mother" and brought to term. The child is called Esmeralda. What will she then pass on ?

My science is only good enough to ask questions, but it seems to me that many questions are left hanging here, from what new paperwork, certificates and forms are needed, to thoughts of the legal rights of various mothers, the child's right concerning inheritances, the medical side of inherited illnesses, and whether I should just sell blank sheets of paper for folk to figure out their Trees on (with help from this book) ? Oh, yes, and should that last egg be christened, and added to the now very lop-sided Tree ?

ONTO THE FUTURE

I've shown in my books "Papertrees" and "Creativitree", and this Memorytrees collection that you can organise the same information in several different ways. Not only that, but I've shown examples of how you can use generic and family specific decoration of literally any subject or design from scrollwork to dinosaurs to trucks, cartoon figures, or computers. Plus I hope that I have shown in this book that, utilising both modern printed materials as well as other found stuff, anyone can create a decent Tree, or some form of chart. Others have demonstrated how to make scrapbooks and memory albums, and it's not a long stretch of imagination to come up with Birthday, Wedding, Christmas etc. cards, certificates, and more.

Of course, if you are artistic, then you should be able to follow all of the above ideas, but draw, paint, etc. the designs. A wrought iron gate in the shape of your Tree ? Very nice. Name tiles on the wall above the bath ? Very contemplative. I can visualise a thousand more, and I'm sure that there are a million possibilities when other folk join in. Trees are a legacy. I have no children, so my writing, music and art has to take that place, but for most folk a filled in Tree is a little piece of yourself to pass on....and we all want to live forever.

Computers are a growing part of the Future, and they can successfully be used for designing Trees. Starting with a graph paper style grid, it is easy to make the boxes. Any of the designs in this book still apply, and you can use clip-art cds plus scanned pictures etc. All of the same Themes are still available, and you may end up doing a Tree for everyone in the family, a cheap but valuable gift.

Who knows, we may one day use holograms and videos clips to end up with a 3-D Tree, with ancestors waving and smiling from their branch. Genealogy is a serious business, but doesn't stop you having fun with your material....anything to help it be remembered and preserved.

Check copyright limitations on what you use. Most folk won't mind you doing a copy for grandma and your cousin, that's personal use, but if you get into mass production and selling stuff with others' artwork on it then you could get into trouble, unless you get permission or it is copyright free. Check first, but there is so much available that you'll be able to find acceptable alternatives.

You can work in black and white, and get the result blown up bigger on a copier. Even colour designs can go onto a disc and be blown up at a copy shop. Mind you, the old ways still work. You could make a clay/wood/metal sculpture of a tree, and hang little framed photos on the branches. Family Trees are both universal, and personal. I wonder what your's will look like........?

Tony Matthews, born 7th May 1949 near Bracknell, Berks, England, second son of George Matthews and Joyce (Cooke) Matthews. Now living in Texas, he designs and sells decorative Family Trees, and his books, through various shops, vendors and societies, and the website www.grillyourgranny.com. He also does articles and talks on Tree designs.

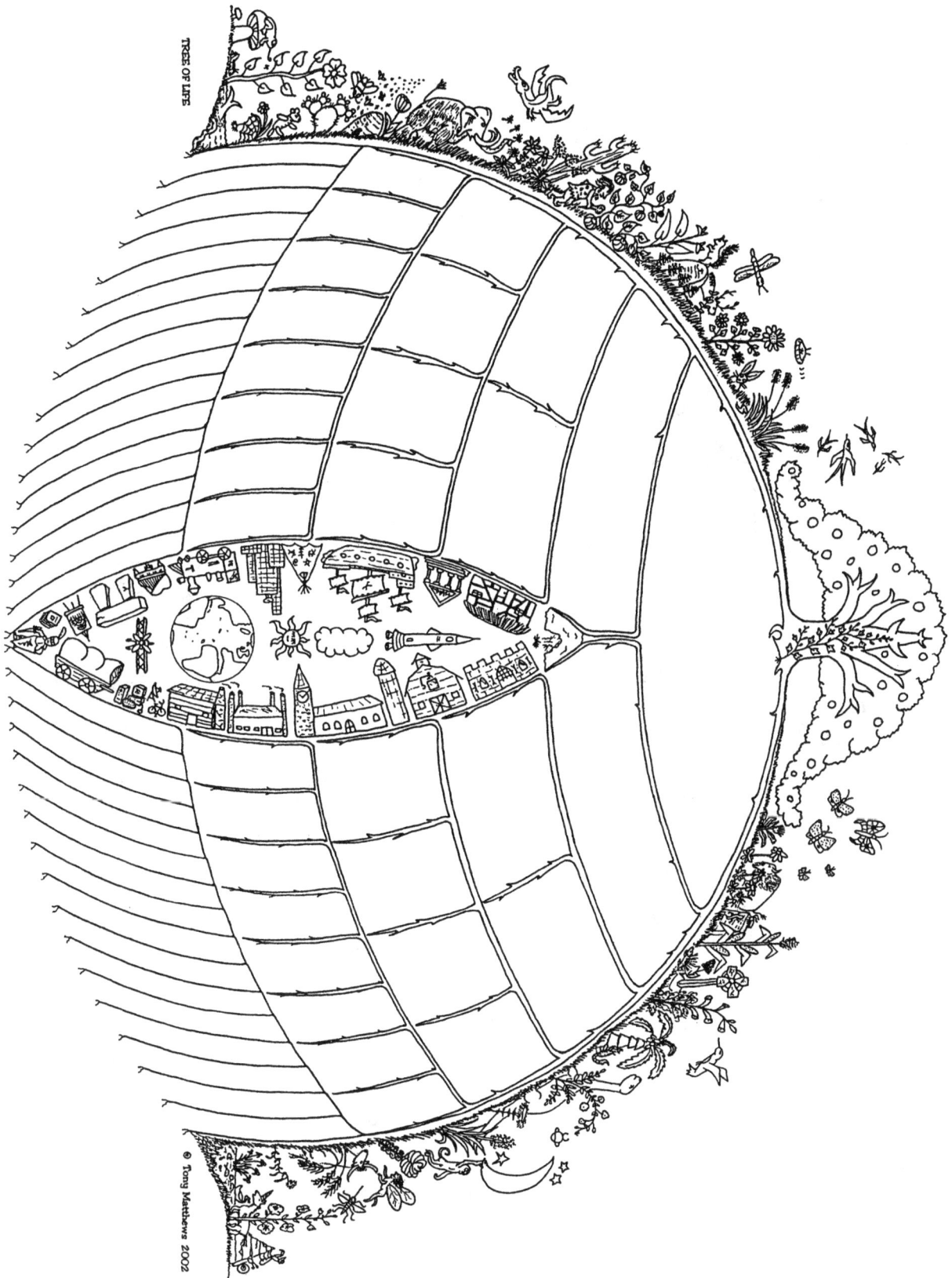

TREE OF LIFE

© Tony Matthews 2002

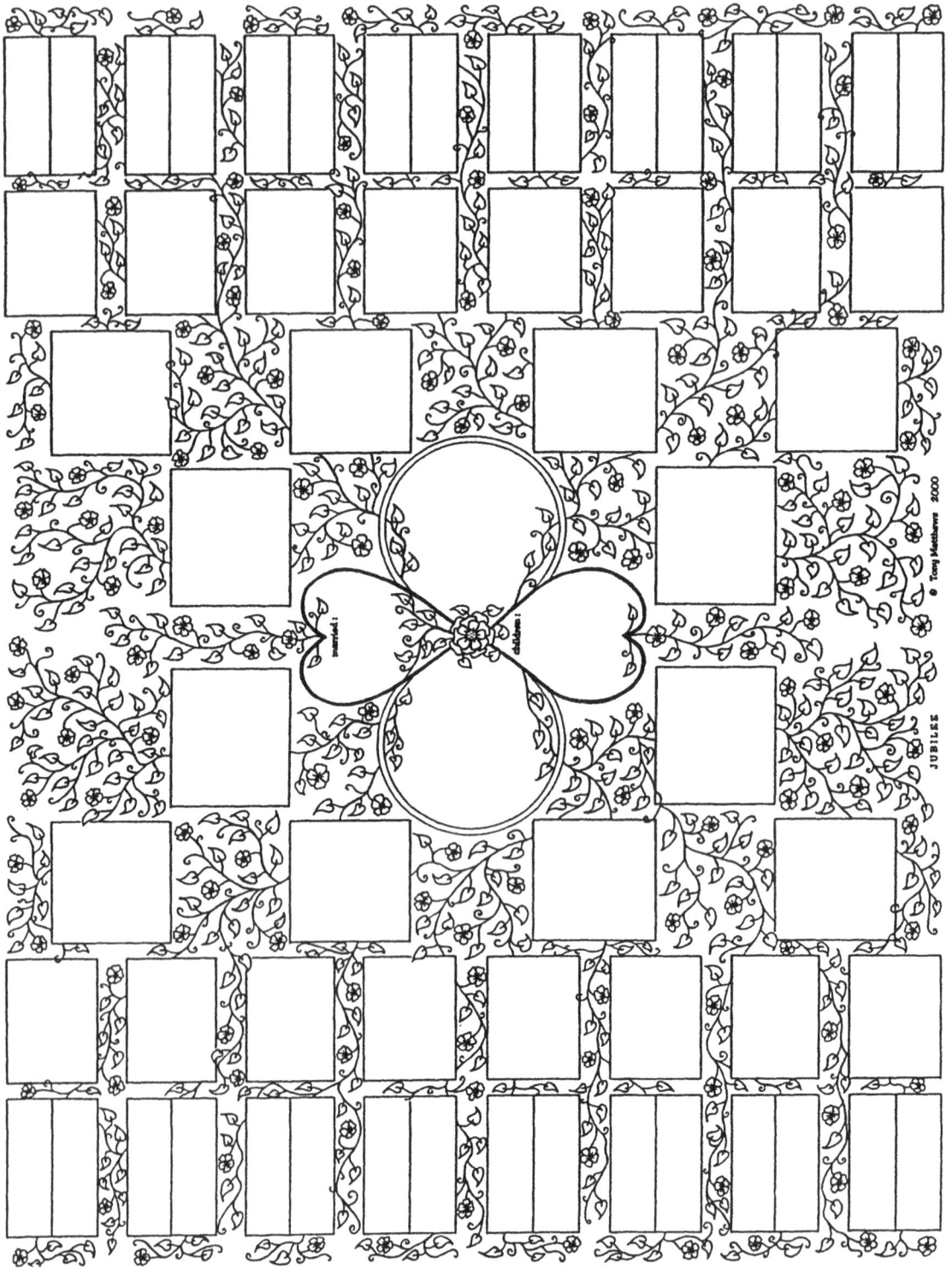

married !

children !

JUBILEE

© Tony Matthews 2000